EMMANUEL JOSEPH

Effective Administration Construction Toolbox For Impact Driven Administrators

Copyright © 2025 by Emmanuel Joseph

All rights reserved. No part of this publication may be reproduced, stored or transmitted in any form or by any means, electronic, mechanical, photocopying, recording, scanning, or otherwise without written permission from the publisher. It is illegal to copy this book, post it to a website, or distribute it by any other means without permission.

First edition

This book was professionally typeset on Reedsy. Find out more at reedsy.com

Contents

1	Chapter 1: Introduction to Effective Administration...	1
2	Chapter 2: Foundations of Organizational Structure	3
3	Chapter 3: Strategic Planning and Implementation	6
4	Chapter 4: Effective Communication Channels	9
5	Chapter 5: Human Resource Management	12
6	Chapter 6: Financial Management and Budgeting	14
7	Chapter 7: Technology and Innovation in Administration	16
8	Chapter 8: Change Management and Adaptability	18
9	Chapter 9: Performance Measurement and Evaluation	20
10	Chapter 10: Legal and Ethical Considerations	22
11	Chapter 11: Leadership and Governance	24
12	Chapter 12: Future Trends in Administration	26

1

Chapter 1: Introduction to Effective Administration Construction

Defining Effective Administration
Effective administration is the bedrock of any successful organization. It involves the systematic and efficient management of resources, processes, and personnel to achieve organizational goals. Effective administration goes beyond mere maintenance of order; it fosters an environment where innovation, productivity, and growth can thrive. Understanding the principles and practices that underpin effective administration enables organizations to build strong foundations that support long-term success and resilience.

Importance of Effective Administration

The significance of effective administration cannot be overstated. In a rapidly evolving world, organizations must be agile and adaptable to survive and prosper. Effective administration provides the structure and processes that enable organizations to respond to challenges and seize opportunities. It ensures that resources are utilized efficiently, that employees are motivated and engaged, and that goals are met in a timely and cost-effective manner. Without effective administration, organizations are likely to experience chaos, inefficiency, and ultimately, failure.

Key Components of Effective Administration

Effective administration comprises several key components, including clear organizational structure, strategic planning, effective communication, and sound financial management. Each of these components plays a critical role in ensuring that an organization runs smoothly and achieves its objectives. A clear organizational structure ensures that roles and responsibilities are well-defined, reducing confusion and increasing accountability. Strategic planning provides a roadmap for the organization's future, guiding decision-making and resource allocation. Effective communication ensures that information flows smoothly within the organization, fostering collaboration and alignment. Sound financial management ensures that resources are used wisely and that the organization remains financially healthy.

Challenges in Achieving Effective Administration

Achieving effective administration is not without its challenges. Organizations often face obstacles such as resistance to change, lack of resources, and conflicting priorities. Resistance to change can stem from employees' fear of the unknown or attachment to the status quo. Lack of resources, whether financial, human, or technological, can hinder the implementation of effective administrative practices. Conflicting priorities can arise when different departments or stakeholders have different goals or perspectives. Overcoming these challenges requires strong leadership, clear communication, and a commitment to continuous improvement.

Paragraph 5: The Role of Leadership in Effective Administration

Leadership plays a pivotal role in effective administration. Leaders set the tone for the organization, shaping its culture and values. They are responsible for making strategic decisions, motivating employees, and ensuring that the organization stays on course to achieve its goals. Effective leaders possess a combination of vision, empathy, and resilience. They inspire and empower their teams, fostering a sense of ownership and accountability. By demonstrating a commitment to excellence and ethical behavior, leaders create an environment where effective administration can flourish.

2

Chapter 2: Foundations of Organizational Structure

The Importance of Organizational Structure

An effective organizational structure is fundamental to the success of any organization. It determines how roles, responsibilities, and authority are distributed, influencing how tasks are coordinated and how information flows. A well-designed organizational structure can enhance efficiency, foster innovation, and improve communication. It provides a clear framework within which employees can operate, reducing confusion and increasing accountability. By understanding the importance of organizational structure, organizations can create an environment that supports their strategic objectives and promotes sustainable growth.

Types of Organizational Structures

There are several types of organizational structures, each with its own advantages and disadvantages. The most common types include functional, divisional, matrix, and flat structures. A functional structure organizes employees based on their specialized skills and functions, such as marketing, finance, and human resources. A divisional structure groups employees based on products, services, or geographical regions. A matrix structure combines elements of both functional and divisional structures, creating a grid-like framework that allows for flexibility and collaboration. A flat structure, on the other hand, has few hierarchical levels, promoting a more open and communicative environment. Understanding these different types of structures allows organizations to choose the one that best suits their needs and goals.

Designing an Effective Organizational Structure

Designing an effective organizational structure involves careful consideration of several factors, including the organization's size, goals, and culture. It requires a thorough analysis of the organization's processes, workflows, and communication channels. The structure should be flexible enough to adapt to changes in the external environment, yet stable enough to provide consistency and predictability. It should also align with the organization's strategic objectives, supporting its mission and vision. Involving employees in the design process can help ensure that the structure is practical and meets the needs of those who will be using it.

Implementing Organizational Structure Changes

Implementing changes to an organizational structure can be challenging. It requires careful planning, clear communication, and strong leadership. Leaders must clearly articulate the reasons for the change and how it will benefit the organization. They must also address any concerns or resistance from employees, providing support and resources to help them adapt to the new structure. Effective implementation involves not only making changes to the organizational chart but also aligning processes, workflows, and communication channels with the new structure. Continuous monitoring and evaluation are essential to ensure that the changes are achieving the desired outcomes.

Paragraph 5: Evaluating and Improving Organizational Structure

Evaluating the effectiveness of an organizational structure is an ongoing process. It involves regularly assessing the structure's impact on efficiency, communication, and employee satisfaction. Organizations should gather feedback from employees and other stakeholders to identify any issues or areas for improvement. They should also stay abreast of changes in the external environment, such as market trends and technological advancements, that may necessitate adjustments to the structure. By continuously evaluating and improving their organizational structure, organizations can ensure that it remains aligned with their strategic objectives and supports their long-term success.

3

Chapter 3: Strategic Planning and Implementation

The Role of Strategic Planning

Strategic planning is a crucial component of effective administration. It involves defining the organization's long-term goals and identifying the best strategies to achieve them. A well-developed strategic plan provides a clear direction for the organization, aligning resources and efforts towards common objectives. It helps organizations anticipate future challenges and opportunities, enabling them to make informed decisions and take proactive measures. By engaging in strategic planning, organizations can ensure that they remain focused on their mission and vision, while also adapting to changing circumstances.

Steps in the Strategic Planning Process

The strategic planning process typically involves several key steps. The first step is conducting a thorough analysis of the organization's internal and external environment. This includes assessing the organization's strengths, weaknesses, opportunities, and threats (SWOT analysis), as well as understanding the competitive landscape and market trends. The next step is setting clear and achievable goals that align with the organization's mission and vision. Once the goals are established, the organization must develop strategies and action plans to achieve them. This involves identifying

CHAPTER 3: STRATEGIC PLANNING AND IMPLEMENTATION

the resources, timelines, and responsibilities required for implementation. Finally, the organization must establish mechanisms for monitoring and evaluating progress, making adjustments as needed to stay on track.

Importance of Stakeholder Involvement

Involving stakeholders in the strategic planning process is essential for its success. Stakeholders include employees, customers, suppliers, investors, and other parties who have an interest in the organization's activities. Engaging stakeholders helps to ensure that the strategic plan reflects diverse perspectives and addresses the needs and expectations of those affected by the organization's decisions. It also fosters a sense of ownership and commitment among stakeholders, increasing the likelihood of successful implementation. Effective communication and collaboration with stakeholders throughout the planning process can lead to more informed decision-making and a stronger, more cohesive strategy.

Challenges in Strategic Planning and Implementation

Strategic planning and implementation are not without challenges. One common challenge is resistance to change, which can hinder the adoption of new strategies and practices. This resistance may stem from employees' fear of the unknown or discomfort with altering established routines. Another challenge is the alignment of resources and priorities. Organizations must ensure that they have the necessary resources, including financial, human, and technological, to execute their strategic plans. Additionally, they must align their priorities to avoid conflicting goals and ensure that efforts are focused on achieving the most critical objectives. Addressing these challenges requires strong leadership, clear communication, and a commitment to continuous improvement.

Paragraph 5: Measuring and Evaluating Strategic Success

Measuring and evaluating the success of strategic planning and implementation is essential for continuous improvement. Organizations must establish key performance indicators (KPIs) to track progress towards their goals. These indicators should be specific, measurable, achievable, relevant, and time-bound (SMART). Regularly reviewing and analyzing performance data allows organizations to identify areas of success and areas needing improvement. It also enables them to make data-driven decisions and adjustments to their strategies and action plans. By continuously measuring and evaluating their strategic efforts, organizations can ensure that they remain on course to achieve their long-term goals and adapt to changing circumstances.

4

Chapter 4: Effective Communication Channels

The Importance of Communication in Administration

Effective communication is a cornerstone of successful administration. It facilitates the flow of information within the organization, enabling employees to collaborate, make informed decisions, and execute their tasks efficiently. Clear and open communication helps to build trust and foster a positive organizational culture. It also ensures that everyone is aligned with the organization's goals and objectives. By prioritizing effective communication, organizations can enhance productivity, innovation, and employee satisfaction.

Types of Communication Channels

There are various communication channels that organizations can utilize to facilitate the exchange of information. These channels can be broadly categorized into formal and informal channels. Formal communication channels include official reports, meetings, memos, and emails. These channels are used to convey important information and directives from management to employees and vice versa. Informal communication channels, on the other hand, include casual conversations, social interactions, and informal feedback. These channels play a crucial role in building relationships, fostering collaboration, and creating a supportive work environment.

Choosing the Right Communication Channels

Selecting the appropriate communication channels is essential for ensuring that messages are effectively conveyed and understood. The choice of channel depends on several factors, including the nature of the message, the intended audience, and the urgency of the communication. For instance, complex or sensitive information may be best communicated through face-to-face meetings or video conferences, where non-verbal cues can enhance understanding. On the other hand, routine updates or announcements can be efficiently conveyed through emails or internal newsletters. By carefully considering the context and purpose of the communication, organizations can select the most suitable channels to achieve their communication goals.

Overcoming Communication Barriers

Effective communication can be hindered by various barriers, including language differences, cultural misunderstandings, and technological limitations. Language differences can lead to misinterpretations and confusion, particularly in organizations with diverse workforces. Cultural misunderstandings can arise from different communication styles, norms, and expectations. Technological limitations, such as unreliable internet connections or outdated communication tools, can also impede the flow of information. To overcome these barriers, organizations must invest in language and cultural training, promote inclusive communication practices, and ensure that they have the necessary technology infrastructure in place.

Paragraph 5: Continuous Improvement of Communication Practices

Continuous improvement of communication practices is vital for maintaining effective administration. Organizations should regularly assess their communication channels and processes to identify areas for enhancement. This can be achieved through feedback surveys, performance evaluations, and communication audits. By involving employees in the process and encouraging open dialogue, organizations can gain valuable insights and make data-driven improvements. Additionally, staying updated on new communication technologies and trends can help organizations adapt to changing communication needs and preferences. By continuously improving their communication practices, organizations can ensure that they remain

CHAPTER 4: EFFECTIVE COMMUNICATION CHANNELS

effective, agile, and responsive to the needs of their stakeholders.

5

Chapter 5: Human Resource Management

The Role of Human Resource Management

Human resource management (HRM) is a critical function in effective administration. It involves the strategic management of an organization's workforce to achieve its goals and objectives. HRM encompasses a wide range of activities, including recruitment, training, performance management, and employee relations. By effectively managing human resources, organizations can attract and retain top talent, develop employee skills, and create a positive work environment. HRM plays a vital role in ensuring that the organization has the right people in the right roles, contributing to overall organizational success.

Recruitment and Selection

Recruitment and selection are key components of HRM. The recruitment process involves identifying and attracting qualified candidates to fill job vacancies. This can be achieved through various methods, such as job postings, employee referrals, and recruitment agencies. Once potential candidates are identified, the selection process involves evaluating their skills, experience, and fit with the organization's culture. This typically includes interviews, assessments, and reference checks. By implementing effective recruitment and selection practices, organizations can ensure that they hire individuals who have the necessary skills and qualities to contribute to their success.

Employee Training and Development

CHAPTER 5: HUMAN RESOURCE MANAGEMENT

Employee training and development are essential for maintaining a skilled and motivated workforce. Training programs provide employees with the knowledge and skills they need to perform their jobs effectively. Development initiatives, on the other hand, focus on enhancing employees' long-term career prospects and personal growth. This can include leadership development, mentorship programs, and opportunities for continuous learning. By investing in training and development, organizations can improve employee performance, boost job satisfaction, and foster a culture of continuous improvement.

Performance Management

Performance management is a systematic approach to evaluating and improving employee performance. It involves setting clear performance goals, providing regular feedback, and conducting performance appraisals. Effective performance management helps to ensure that employees are aligned with the organization's objectives and are motivated to achieve their best. It also provides a framework for recognizing and rewarding high performers, as well as identifying areas for improvement and providing support and resources for development. By implementing a robust performance management system, organizations can enhance productivity, employee engagement, and overall organizational performance.

Paragraph 5: Employee Relations and Engagement

Maintaining positive employee relations and engagement is crucial for creating a supportive and productive work environment. Employee relations involve managing the relationship between the organization and its employees, addressing any issues or conflicts that arise. Engagement, on the other hand, refers to the level of commitment and enthusiasm employees have towards their work and the organization. By fostering open communication, providing opportunities for employee involvement, and recognizing and rewarding contributions, organizations can build strong employee relations and enhance engagement. This, in turn, leads to increased job satisfaction, reduced turnover, and improved organizational performance.

6

Chapter 6: Financial Management and Budgeting

Financial Reporting and Analysis

Financial reporting and analysis are critical for maintaining transparency and accountability within an organization. Financial reports, such as balance sheets, income statements, and cash flow statements, provide a comprehensive view of the organization's financial health. Analyzing these reports helps organizations identify trends, monitor performance, and make informed decisions. By regularly reviewing financial reports, organizations can detect potential issues early and take corrective actions to ensure financial stability and growth.

Risk Management and Mitigation

Risk management is an essential aspect of financial management. It involves identifying, assessing, and prioritizing potential risks that could impact the organization's financial health. These risks can include market fluctuations, economic downturns, and operational disruptions. By developing and implementing risk mitigation strategies, organizations can minimize the impact of these risks and protect their financial resources. This may involve diversifying investments, purchasing insurance, and establishing contingency plans. Effective risk management helps organizations navigate uncertainties and maintain financial resilience.

CHAPTER 6: FINANCIAL MANAGEMENT AND BUDGETING

Paragraph 5: The Role of Financial Managers

Financial managers play a crucial role in effective financial management. They are responsible for overseeing the organization's financial activities, developing budgets, and ensuring compliance with financial regulations. Financial managers also provide strategic insights and recommendations to support decision-making and drive organizational growth. By leveraging their expertise in financial analysis, planning, and risk management, financial managers help organizations achieve their financial objectives and sustain long-term success.

7

Chapter 7: Technology and Innovation in Administration

Embracing Technological Advancements

In the modern era, technology plays a pivotal role in effective administration. Organizations must embrace technological advancements to streamline processes, enhance productivity, and stay competitive. This includes adopting software solutions for project management, communication, and data analysis. By leveraging technology, organizations can automate routine tasks, reduce errors, and improve overall efficiency. Embracing technological innovation allows organizations to adapt to changing market conditions and capitalize on new opportunities.

Implementing Digital Transformation

Digital transformation involves integrating digital technologies into all aspects of an organization's operations. This process requires a strategic approach and a commitment to continuous improvement. Implementing digital transformation includes upgrading IT infrastructure, adopting cloud-based solutions, and utilizing data analytics to drive decision-making. Organizations must also invest in employee training to ensure that staff can effectively use new technologies. By successfully implementing digital transformation, organizations can enhance their agility, improve customer experiences, and achieve operational excellence.

Overcoming Technology-Related Challenges

While technology offers numerous benefits, it also presents challenges that organizations must address. These challenges include cybersecurity threats, data privacy concerns, and the potential for technological obsolescence. To overcome these challenges, organizations must develop robust cybersecurity measures, establish data protection policies, and stay updated on emerging technologies. Additionally, fostering a culture of innovation and adaptability can help organizations navigate the complexities of technology adoption and maximize its benefits.

8

Chapter 8: Change Management and Adaptability

The Need for Change Management

In today's dynamic business environment, change is inevitable. Organizations must be prepared to adapt to new market conditions, technological advancements, and evolving customer needs. Change management is the process of guiding an organization through these transitions in a structured and systematic way. Effective change management ensures that changes are implemented smoothly and that employees are supported throughout the process. By prioritizing change management, organizations can minimize disruptions, maintain productivity, and achieve successful outcomes.

Key Principles of Change Management

Successful change management is built on several key principles. These include clear communication, stakeholder involvement, and strong leadership. Clear communication ensures that all employees understand the reasons for the change, the benefits it will bring, and their role in the process. Involving stakeholders in the planning and implementation phases helps to build support and address concerns. Strong leadership provides direction and motivation, helping to guide the organization through the transition. By adhering to these principles, organizations can effectively manage change and achieve their strategic goals.

Building a Culture of Adaptability

Adaptability is a critical trait for organizations in an ever-changing world. Building a culture of adaptability involves fostering a mindset of continuous improvement and encouraging employees to embrace change. This can be achieved through training and development programs, open communication, and recognizing and rewarding innovative ideas. By creating an environment where adaptability is valued, organizations can respond more effectively to new challenges and opportunities, ensuring long-term success and resilience.

9

Chapter 9: Performance Measurement and Evaluation

Importance of Performance Measurement

Performance measurement is essential for assessing the effectiveness of an organization's strategies and operations. By establishing key performance indicators (KPIs) and monitoring progress, organizations can identify areas of success and areas needing improvement. Performance measurement provides valuable insights that inform decision-making and resource allocation. It also promotes accountability and transparency, ensuring that all employees are aligned with the organization's goals and objectives.

Methods of Performance Evaluation

There are various methods for evaluating organizational performance, including financial analysis, balanced scorecards, and employee performance appraisals. Financial analysis involves assessing the organization's financial health through metrics such as revenue, profitability, and return on investment. Balanced scorecards provide a comprehensive view of performance by considering multiple dimensions, such as financial, customer, internal processes, and learning and growth. Employee performance appraisals evaluate individual contributions and identify opportunities for development. By utilizing a combination of these methods, organizations can gain a holistic understanding of their performance.

Continuous Improvement Through Evaluation

Continuous improvement is a key outcome of effective performance measurement and evaluation. By regularly reviewing performance data and seeking feedback from employees and stakeholders, organizations can identify areas for enhancement and implement changes to drive progress. This iterative process fosters a culture of learning and innovation, enabling organizations to adapt to evolving market conditions and achieve their strategic objectives. Through continuous improvement, organizations can maintain a competitive edge and achieve long-term success.

10

Chapter 10: Legal and Ethical Considerations

Importance of Legal Compliance

Legal compliance is a fundamental aspect of effective administration. Organizations must adhere to relevant laws and regulations to avoid legal penalties, protect their reputation, and maintain stakeholder trust. This includes compliance with labor laws, environmental regulations, data protection requirements, and industry-specific standards. By prioritizing legal compliance, organizations can operate ethically and responsibly, minimizing the risk of legal issues and ensuring long-term sustainability.

Ethical Considerations in Administration

Ethical considerations are equally important in administration. Organizations must uphold ethical standards in their decision-making, interactions with stakeholders, and overall conduct. This involves promoting transparency, integrity, and accountability, as well as considering the social and environmental impact of organizational activities. By fostering an ethical culture, organizations can build trust with employees, customers, and the broader community, enhancing their reputation and achieving sustainable success.

Integrating Legal and Ethical Practices

Integrating legal and ethical practices into organizational operations

CHAPTER 10: LEGAL AND ETHICAL CONSIDERATIONS

requires a proactive approach. This includes developing and implementing policies and procedures that promote compliance and ethical behavior. Organizations should also provide regular training and education to employees on legal and ethical issues, ensuring that they understand their responsibilities and the importance of ethical conduct. By embedding legal and ethical considerations into the organizational culture, organizations can create a strong foundation for responsible and sustainable growth.

11

Chapter 11: Leadership and Governance

The Role of Leadership
Leadership is a critical component of effective administration. Leaders set the vision and direction for the organization, inspiring and motivating employees to achieve their best. Effective leaders possess a combination of strategic thinking, emotional intelligence, and resilience. They are able to navigate complex challenges, make informed decisions, and foster a positive organizational culture. By providing strong leadership, organizations can achieve their strategic goals and drive long-term success.

Principles of Good Governance
Good governance is essential for ensuring accountability, transparency, and ethical conduct within an organization. It involves establishing clear roles and responsibilities, implementing robust policies and procedures, and promoting open communication. Good governance practices help to build trust with stakeholders and enhance organizational performance. By adhering to the principles of good governance, organizations can maintain their integrity and achieve sustainable growth.

Building Leadership and Governance Capacity
Building leadership and governance capacity requires a commitment to continuous learning and development. Organizations should invest in leadership development programs, mentorship, and training initiatives to enhance the skills and competencies of their leaders. Additionally, fostering a

culture of collaboration and inclusivity can strengthen governance practices and ensure that diverse perspectives are considered in decision-making. By building leadership and governance capacity, organizations can enhance their resilience and adaptability, positioning themselves for long-term success.

12

Chapter 12: Future Trends in Administration

Technological Advancements

Technological advancements are shaping the future of administration. Innovations such as artificial intelligence, automation, and data analytics are transforming how organizations operate. These technologies offer opportunities to enhance efficiency, improve decision-making, and drive innovation. Organizations must stay updated on emerging technologies and explore how they can be leveraged to achieve their strategic objectives. By embracing technological advancements, organizations can stay competitive and adapt to changing market conditions.

Emphasis on Sustainability

Sustainability is becoming increasingly important in the realm of administration. Organizations are recognizing the need to consider the environmental and social impact of their activities. This involves adopting sustainable practices, such as reducing carbon emissions, conserving resources, and promoting social responsibility. By prioritizing sustainability, organizations can enhance their reputation, attract environmentally-conscious customers, and contribute to the well-being of society. The emphasis on sustainability is likely to continue shaping administrative practices in the future.

Evolving Workforce Dynamics

CHAPTER 12: FUTURE TRENDS IN ADMINISTRATION

Workforce dynamics are evolving, and organizations must adapt to these changes to remain effective. This includes addressing the needs and expectations of a diverse and multi-generational workforce, promoting work-life balance, and embracing remote and flexible work arrangements. Organizations must also invest in employee well-being and development to attract and retain top talent.

Effective Administration Construction

In today's dynamic and complex world, the success of any organization hinges on effective administration. "Effective Administration Construction" provides a comprehensive guide to mastering the art of administration, offering practical insights and strategies for building and maintaining a resilient, efficient, and innovative organization.

This book covers a wide range of topics essential for effective administration, including organizational structure, strategic planning, communication channels, human resource management, financial management, and the integration of technology and innovation. Each chapter delves into the key principles, challenges, and best practices associated with these areas, providing readers with the tools they need to navigate the complexities of modern administration.

Through real-world examples, actionable advice, and a focus on continuous improvement, "Effective Administration Construction" empowers leaders, managers, and administrators to create and sustain high-performing organizations. Whether you're a seasoned executive or new to the field, this book offers valuable insights and practical guidance to help you achieve your goals and drive long-term success.

www.ingramcontent.com/pod-product-compliance
Lightning Source LLC
LaVergne TN
LVHW010444070526
838199LV00066B/6189